WHAT IS OUR HERITAGE?

UNITED KINGDOM COUNCIL
for European Architectural Heritage Year

President
His Royal Highness The Duke of Edinburgh

Vice-Presidents
Rt Hon Anthony Crosland MP
  Secretary of State for the Environment
Rt Hon William Ross MP
  Secretary of State for Scotland
Rt Hon John Morris MP
  Secretary of State for Wales
Rt Hon Merlyn Rees MP
  Secretary of State for Northern Ireland
Mr Timothy Raison MP
Rt Hon Jeremy Thorpe MP
Baroness Birk
  *Parliamentary Under Secretary of State,
  Department of the Environment*

Members
Archbishop of Canterbury
Archbishop of Westminster
Chief Rabbi
Moderator, General Assembly of the Church of
  Scotland
Rev Herbert Simpson, Methodist Church
Sir John Betjeman
Sir Hugh Casson
Lord Clark
Lord Goodman
Lord Kennet
Sir Osbert Lancaster
Mr Henry Moore
Sir James Richards
Dr Roy Strong

The Advertising Association
Ancient Monuments Board (England)
Ancient Monuments Board (Scotland)
Ancient Monuments Board (Wales)
Ancient Monuments Society
Arts Council of Great Britain
Association for the Protection of Rural Scotland
Association of British Chambers of Commerce
Association of County Councils
Association of County Councils in Scotland
Association of District Councils
Association of Education Committees
Association of Metropolitan Authorities
Automobile Association
The British Council
British Property Federation
British Railways Board
British Tourist Authority
British Trust for Conservation Volunteers
British Waterways Board
Building Societies Association
Church Commissioners
Committee for Environmental Conservation
Confederation of British Industry
Convention of Royal Burghs
Council for British Archaeology

Council for the Protection of Rural England
Council for the Protection of Rural Wales
Country Landowners Association
Crown Estate Commissioners
Design Council
Electricity Council
English Tourist Board
European Movement
Georgian Group
Girl Guides Association
Historic Buildings Council for England
Historic Buildings Council for Scotland
Historic Buildings Council for Wales
Historic Monuments Council (Northern Ireland)
Institute of Directors
Institute of Landscape Architects
Institute of Park and Recreation Administration
Institution of Civil Engineers
Institution of Municipal Engineers
Maritime Trust
Multiple Shops Federation
Museums Association
National Association of Boys' Clubs
National Association of Local Councils
National Chamber of Trade
National Council for Voluntary Youth Services
National Council of Social Service
National Federation of Housing Societies
National Federation of Women's Institutes
National Trust
National Trust for Scotland
National Union of Townswomen's Guilds
National Water Council
Northern Ireland Tourist Board
Pilgrim Trust
Post Office
Professional Institutions Council for Conservation
Redundant Churches Fund
Royal Academy of Arts
Royal Automobile Club
Royal Commission on Ancient and Historical
  Monuments of Scotland
Royal Commission on Ancient and Historical
  Monuments, Wales
Royal Commission on Historical Monuments
  (England)
Royal Fine Art Commission
Royal Fine Art Commission for Scotland
Royal Incorporation of Architects in Scotland
Royal Institute of British Architects
Royal Institution of Chartered Surveyors
Royal Society of Arts
Royal Society of Ulster Architects
Royal Town Planning Institute
Scottish Tourist Board
Scout Association
Society for the Protection of Ancient Buildings
Society of Antiquaries of London
Society of Antiquaries of Scotland
Society of Architectural Historians of Great Britain
Standing Commission on Museums and Galleries
Town and Country Planning Association
Trades Union Congress
Transport Trust
Ulster Architectural Heritage Society
Victorian Society
Wales Tourist Board

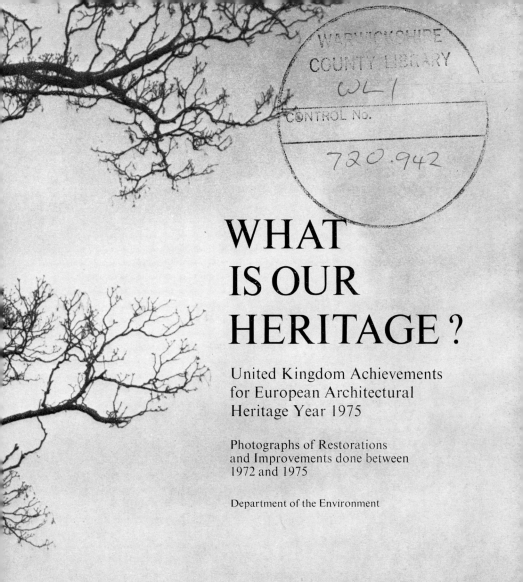

WHAT
IS OUR
HERITAGE ?

United Kingdom Achievements
for European Architectural
Heritage Year 1975

Photographs of Restorations
and Improvements done between
1972 and 1975

Department of the Environment

London Her Majesty's Stationery Office

ISBN 0 11 750908 6

Introduction

BUCKINGHAM PALACE.

There is a compelling fascination about old buildings - how else can one explain the vast throngs of tourists who travel all over the world to look at and to admire the work of architects and craftsmen of every age and culture? Yet many people including, one presumes, a good many tourists, take their own surroundings for granted and only get upset when a familiar landmark disappears to be replaced by something new and strange.

The trouble with architecture is that its creations have to be enjoyed or endured just as much by the public as by the owner. Buildings are a truly national collection of functional and cultural structures, each generation acting as a more or less considerate curator of this record of the progress of national civilisation.

I sometimes suspect that people become intrigued by old buildings because it comes as such a surprise to find that any previous generation could possibly have done anything better than their own. This is particularly true in this generation which seems to think it has invented such ideas as social justice, concern for the poor and the advantages of peace and love. Judging by the indiscriminate destruction of old buildings and their replacement by socially and aesthetically

disastrous structures in recent years, it
suggests a quite remarkable degree of
arrogance and disregard for lessons painfully
learned in previous generations.

The great achievement of European
Architectural Heritage Year has been to draw
attention to the short-comings of our
generation as curators of the European
architectural collection. Curators in the
sense that they are responsible for the
maintenance of the collection and for its
constant up-dating.

The European Architectural Heritage Year
campaign itself has also succeeded in
demonstrating just what can be done with a
little effort, taste and consideration. The
pages of this book record some of the
remarkable successes of the campaign, but it
is really a memorial to Lady Dartmouth and
all the enthusiastic and willing helpers all
over the country who have been responsible
for converting the idea of the European
Architectural Heritage Year into a living
practical program of solid achievement.

1975.

Contents

Front and Back cover: Priory Lane, King's Lynn, Norfolk. *King's Lynn Preservation Trust*
End papers: Gates by Tijou, Drayton House, Northamptonshire. *Lionel Stopford Sackville*
Half Title Page: Castle Combe, Dorset
Title Page: Auchroisk Distillery, Fife. *International Distillers and Vintners*
Reverse of Title Page: Bingley Locks, Bradford. *British Waterways Board*

What is our Heritage?

What is our heritage? Is it the mills of the North, the half-timbered houses of the Midlands, or the thatched cottages of the South? Is it the palace, the church, the railway station, the water tower, the manor or the village green? It is all of them, and the extraordinary variety stimulates the mind and the eye.

When we started to plan our campaign for Heritage Year, at the end of 1972, we decided to concentrate upon three main objectives. First, practical projects. Second, a national revolving fund. Third, environmental education. Today, over thirteen hundred practical projects are completed or under way; the fund has reached £400,000 from private sources, to be backed pound for pound by the Government; and almost every Education Authority throughout England has pledged its support.

The photographs shown on these pages represent the work of private owners, commercial firms, amenity societies, councils, New Towns, electricity boards, and volunteers of all ages. Everyone has helped. Grants from the Government of nearly £3 million were given to outstanding Conservation Areas, such as Chester, or York. Heritage Grants totalling £180,000 were shared by applicants from villages, towns or cities as a percentage of the total cost.

Our Architectural Heritage Fund is designed to save difficult buildings which do not easily sell on the open market. In Fife, over one hundred houses have been bought, restored and resold with protective covenants, by the National Trust for Scotland. Following the same system, our money will be lent at low interest rates to local historic buildings trusts. The capital will then return, on a revolving basis, to be used again in another area.

In the field of Education, many counties have produced heritage guides and other information for use in schools; headmasters have included environmental studies in their curricula; and the enthusiasm of teachers has given this subject a new impetus. Polytechnics and Universities have also co-operated. The South Bank Polytechnic, London, is introducing a degree in the History and Theory of the Built Environment. Students from far and near attended the lectures commissioned by the Royal Society of Arts on different aspects of conservation. Special courses in architectural studies are being held for tutors and interested adults. The educational supplement of Heritage Year News has now reached a circulation of 38,000 copies.

So much for our three main aims. Other problems emerged. Legislation needed tightening to prevent demolition in Conservation Areas, and for greater control over unsuitable advertisements and shop fascias. This has been covered by the Town and Country Amenities Act 1974, and Circular 102 urges Local Authorities to appoint a Conservation Officer within their planning departments.

In the public and private sector the emphasis has shifted from destruction to rehabilitation. Sometimes this is cheaper. Greater London Council figures show comparable savings of 10–15% per dwelling as well as substantial economies in raw materials. When restoration is more expensive grants should be larger, as in Holland, where owners can claim up to 80%, divided between the Government and the municipality. We hope that our Government will consider continuing the enhancement grants for non-outstanding Conservation Areas, as this incentive is a proven success.

The shortage of both student and post-graduate conservation courses for architects should be remedied without delay. Equally the conservation craftsman deserves special training and recognition within the building industry. Business and Industry should place greater emphasis on environmental values, within the context of maintaining a prosperous economy.

In the final analysis, successful conservation depends upon: the right climate of public opinion, the necessary legislation and the will to use those powers, money from both public and private sources, and the skill to implement imaginative schemes. For European Architectural Heritage Year we in the United Kingdom have tried to combine all these factors. We found goodwill in plenty. We also found that people have a deep-seated desire to preserve our links with the past and to give them a new role in the future. It is the next generation who will judge our success or failure. Meanwhile we shall strive to achieve the rebirth of historic buildings and historic areas, which give us a feeling of continuity and a sense of security, only derived from the familiar and the loved, to help us face the difficult years which lie ahead.

1. Before and After

Sometimes it is almost impossible to believe the evidence that buildings which were literally falling to pieces have been given a new lease of life. Ruined castles in Spain, 'hotels' of the nobility in the Marais 'degradés' by dilapidated sheds and workshops in their crumbling courtyards, gabled houses with insecure foundations along the canals of Amsterdam, all have been restored with sensitivity and meticulous attention to detail. It took time, money and imagination. Most important of all was the will to win.

Unique in Britain is our industrial heritage. In contrast to the romantic moulin-a-vent of Alphonse Daudet in Provence, we have the sternly practical flour mills of the south, and the cotton mills of Yorkshire, Lancashire and Derbyshire which dominate their northern skylines. No longer dark and satanic, many have become offices or homes, and the entire mill village of New Lanark in Scotland, where the walls are a foot thick, is gradually being modernised. Preston Oatmeal Mill, at East Linton, with a tiled roof, where swans glide on a nearby pond, is a more gentle reminder of our industrial past; the waterworks at Perth and the pumping station at Ryhope, Sunderland, are exciting and unusual. At Darlington, where the first passenger railway linked Stockton with the midlands, the station has been carefully restored, and Monkwearmouth Station, an elegant building of 1848, is now a transport museum.

In some areas groups of buildings have the greatest impact, and extensive improvements have taken place in Delph, a former mining village in the Pennines, and Firwood Fold, Bolton, birthplace of Samuel Crompton who invented the Spinning Mule.

In contrast, streets of seventeenth and eighteenth century shops and houses have been saved at Faversham, in Kent, and at Coleshill and Alcester in Warwickshire. The photograph of Lansdowne Parade, Cheltenham, shows one example of the hundreds of restored villas or terraces, some with intricate iron balconies or window canopies, which are such an interesting survival of Regency town planning.

Buildings can only survive if people care enough. We salute all the private individuals, and members of local authorities or amenity societies who had the courage of their convictions.

Castle Mill, Dorking, Surrey, listed in the Doomsday Book, now a private house.
Derek Morrison-Jones

4

Six-sail stone windmill at Heage, circa 1850.
Derbyshire County Council

Exciting discovery of 18th Century Adam house beneath Victorian exterior. Kelso, Scotland.
Lady Biddulph

Clever mixture of old and new; five homes and a shop.
Norwich Preservation Trust

Perth Waterworks, 1832, with cast-iron dome and cistern, now a Tourist Centre.
The Town Council of the City and Royal Burgh of Perth

16th Century house with heraldic crests, now a restaurant.
William Lovell, Exeter, Devon

12

Modernisation and new uses in High Street, Coleshill.
North Warwickshire Borough Council

Dramatic rescue of The Crescent, Buxton, now the public library and offices.
Derbyshire County Council

16th Century Pitcullo Castle, Fife.
Roy Spence

One of twenty-three small-scale Regency terrace houses in Lansdowne Parade, Cheltenham, restored by different owners. *Cheltenham Borough Council*

Mediaeval street at Alcester, Warwickshire, now old people's housing.
Stratford-upon-Avon District Council

2. Details

We are often dazzled by fine architecture—by the grandeur of St Peters, by the sweeping facade of Castle Howard, by our first view of the Place Stanislas at Nancy. Yet it is sometimes the details that we remember most. We see in our mind's eye the gargoyles of Notre Dame, the mosaics at Daphni, the gilded pulpit at Wurzburg, and the wrought-iron of the Alabaster Mosque in Cairo.

In this country several of our distinguished architects were also decorators. Adam designed furniture subsequently made by Chippendale, and employed Zucchi and Angelica Kaufmann to paint their exquisite panels and overdoors. Holland used Pernotin for decorative work at Althorp and for George IV at Carlton House. Charles Rennie Mackintosh designed every table and chair of Miss Cranston's famous tea rooms in Glasgow, and even the rose-coloured stained glass for the main bedroom in Hill House, Helensburgh.

It is difficult nowadays to find skilled craftsmen and stonemasons to repair and renew such delicate work, and more training schemes for this purpose are urgently required. In Spain, local craft workshops are set up in villages to make latches, hinges and other ironwork for the Paradors, former palaces or castles now converted into government hotels.

Can we learn from this idea? Prince Philip has suggested that people whose hobbies are related to conservation, might extend their activities into weekend or part-time work. Some local authorities, who hold evening classes which teach anything from millinery to learning Italian, could perhaps include special courses in practical restoration. In the following photographs you will see a few examples of decorative details which contribute so much to the whole—I wish I could also show you the fireplace of the three wise monkeys by Burges at Tower House, Kensington; the Hawkesmoor ceiling in the Library of Queens College, Oxford; the pargeting on early houses in Essex; and the many surprising, funny, fantastic or beautiful details which abound in our architecture whether on grand mansions or more humble buildings up and down the country.

Carolean staircase in carved oak at Tyttenhanger House, Hertfordshire, now architects' offices.
John S Bonnington Partnership

22

Chair from Hill House, Helensburgh, built and furnished by Mackintosh, circa 1900.
Royal Incorporation of Architects in Scotland

Stone vase of 1830 on the Fowler building, Covent Garden.
Greater London Council

24

Norton Priory undercroft, dating from 1134, showing Georgian wine racks.
Runcorn Development Corporation

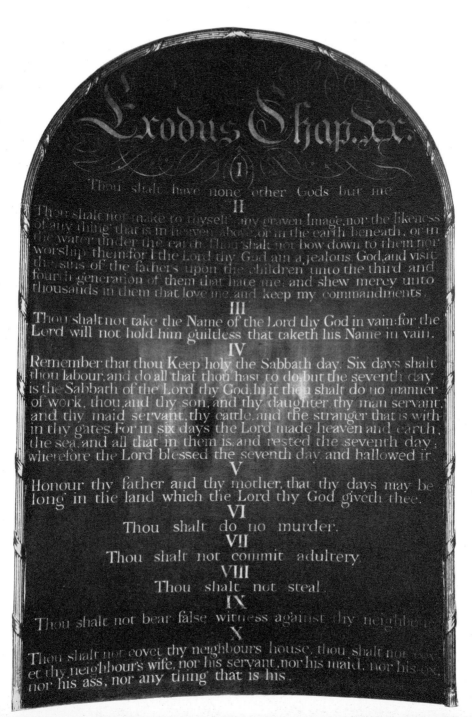

25

18th Century Tablet above the Holy Table at the Geffrye Museum Chapel, Shoreditch.
Greater London Council

Exodus Chap.xx.

I

Thou shalt have none other Gods but me.

II

Thou shalt not make to thyself any graven Image, nor the likeness of any thing that is in heaven above, or in the earth beneath, or in the water under the earth. Thou shalt not bow down to them nor worship them: for I the Lord thy God am a jealous God, and visit the sins of the fathers upon the children unto the third and fourth generation of them that hate me; and shew mercy unto thousands in them that love me, and keep my commandments.

III

Thou shalt not take the Name of the Lord thy God in vain: for the Lord will not hold him guiltless that taketh his Name in vain.

IV

Remember that thou Keep holy the Sabbath day. Six days shalt thou labour, and do all that thou hast to do: but the seventh day is the Sabbath of the Lord thy God: in it thou shalt do no manner of work, thou, and thy son, and thy daughter, thy man servant, and thy maid servant, thy cattle, and the stranger that is within thy gates. For in six days the Lord made heaven and earth, the sea, and all that in them is, and rested the seventh day; wherefore the Lord blessed the seventh day and hallowed it.

V

Honour thy father and thy mother, that thy days may be long in the land which the Lord thy God giveth thee.

VI

Thou shalt do no murder.

VII

Thou shalt not commit adultery.

VIII

Thou shalt not steal.

IX

Thou shalt not bear false witness against thy neighbour.

X

Thou shalt not covet thy neighbours house, thou shalt not covet thy neighbour's wife, nor his servant, nor his maid, nor his ox, nor his ass, nor any thing that is his.

26

Ceiling of the Lake Pavilion, by John Vanbrugh, 1717, at Stowe, Buckinghamshire.
Governors of Stowe School

Staircase in building designed for the Port of London Authority by Edwin Cooper, 1922.
Amalgamated Investments

Craftsman working on Adam panel at Kenwood House, Hampstead.
Greater London Council

Door canopies of 1703 at Laurence Pountney Hill, City.
Haslemere Estates

Regency chandelier at 16, Carlton House Terrace, London.
Crockford's Club

3. New Uses

Buildings are for people. It is sad to see an historic house beautifully restored, yet, like many of the chateaux of the Loire, echoing, not to the sound of family life, but only to the casual tread of tourists. Buildings transplanted into open-air museums, such as St Fagans, outside Cardiff, or Singleton in Sussex, are useful for history lessons, and provide such delights as a gipsy caravan, a tannery, and a charcoal burner's hut, but there is an air of unreality. I felt the same at the Escorial, in Spain, where paintings intended for the muted atmosphere of a baptistery or a chapel had been re-hung on the glaring white walls of a newly-created gallery.

Since 1967, when legislation to preserve historic buildings has been increasingly strengthened by successive Governments, more ingenuity has been used in the United Kingdom to invent new uses for mansions, prisons, churches, warehouses, mills and even lavatories.

It is obviously easier for local authorities or commercial undertakings to bear the heavy cost of conversions, and we feel that private individuals should be helped to a greater extent. There are powers under the Historic Buildings Act 1962 for Councils to give grants, but they are not obliged to do so. In Holland, up to 80% can be claimed automatically, half from the municipality and half from national funds.

Despite financial problems and requirements of building acts and fire regulations which can spoil architectural features like doors or ceilings, thousands of unlikely buildings are now shops, offices, community centres or homes.

People often prefer working in the special atmosphere of old buildings, provided they have modern services. This was emphasised to me on recent visits to Droitwich, Worcestershire, where a typical half-timbered house is now an architects' office, and in Banbury, Oxfordshire, where a Tudor house with rare pargeting has been sensitively converted by a building society. The employees at Sainsbury's headquarters near Blackfriars Bridge are rightly proud of their luxurious basement canteen, seating three hundred and fifty, formerly a cheese store, and I hope that the other examples we show of successful new uses will encourage the timid to even greater originality.

Once a tannery store, West Mill, Edinburgh, circa 1805, is now twenty-two modern flats.
Link Housing Association

32

Formerly a prison and police barracks, this Georgian building in Bath is now twelve flats. *Bath City Council*

Samlesbury Hall, circa 1400, with later additions, now cleverly converted to a theatre and craft centre. Mellor. *Samlesbury Hall Trustees and CPRE Lancashire*

Endowed by William de Montfichet in 1134. The Clock Flour-mill, Bromley-by-Bow, London, is now offices and bottling plant. *Bass Charrington Vintners*

Exceat Farm, built of flint and brick in the 18th Century, now a countryside Interpretive Centre, Seaford. *East Sussex County Council*

This Victorian Chapel in Lincoln is now an architect's office.
Palmer and Holland

36

The Ivory House, St Katherine Dock, London, one of the splendid warehouses designed by Aitchison and Telford in the 1820's. Now flats overlooking the yacht marina. *Taylor Woodrow*

The Old Town Hall, built by a Recorder of Westbury, Wiltshire, in 1815, now shops and offices. *Sandoe and Sandoe*

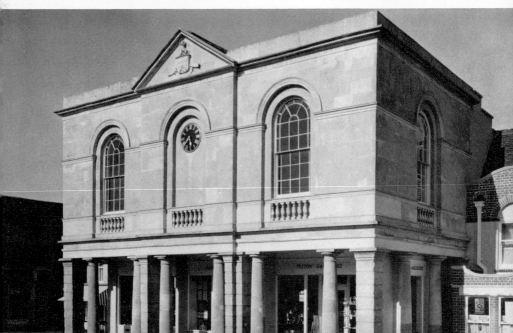

Built in 1386 as a common latrine, now used for lectures and parties.
Warden and Scholars, New College, Oxford

Dedicated to St Thomas of Canterbury after completion in 1190, this chapel at Ludlow is now a house. *South Shropshire District Council*

Kenilworth Water Tower, Warwickshire, circa 1778, originally a windmill, now a private house. *Michael Wheat*

4. Beauty Restored

It was, ironically, from the first floor windows of the Banqueting House, built for pleasure, as part of the grand design of the uncompleted Whitehall Palace, that Charles I stepped on to the scaffold. It was in the romantic Temple of Diana, at Blenheim, that Winston Churchill proposed to the beautiful Clementine Hozier. It was at Dover, when the scare of invasion by Napoleon was mounting in 1812, that Crabble Mill was built to provide flour for the troops.

Not all the buildings in these pages have such a dramatic history, but the Dovecote with six hundred nesting boxes at Cumbernauld, and the small house with unusual plasterwork sold for five shillings in 1702, represent the modest but charming buildings which are the essential back-drop to those which dominate the centre of the stage. Almshouses and a church, both part of everyday life, are here dramatised by their architecture. Bodley's polychromatic decoration has an unearthly glow, while the turrets, gables and heraldic beasts of the Watermen's Asylum at Penge conjure up Camelot.

It is easy to argue that all this is irrelevant in the nuclear age, but anyone who has seen, in newer countries, mile upon mile of brash new blocks interspersed only by crude advertisements, and where people are no happier, will echo Jane Jacobs on the basic need for old buildings, in her study of 'The Death and Life of Great American Cities'.

Perhaps it is unimportant that the same family have owned and lived in the same house since the Norman Conquest? Yet it means that they have cared for it and repaired it, and made financial sacrifices to hand it on to the next generation. Nowadays nearly all our stately homes are enjoyed by the public. They can wander at will in the gardens, admire the paintings and furniture, and have tea in former stables or orangeries. When the family are still there the house is loved, private money is still spent on improvements, and it is not just another debit entry in the accounts of the Local Authority.

Grand or humble, thousands of our historic buildings still have a useful life.

Egyptian Revival house, circa 1830, Penzance, Cornwall, now three flats.
Landmark Trust

42

Polychromatic decoration by George Frederick Bodley, circa 1871, in St John the Baptist Church, Liverpool. *Vicar and Churchwardens*

Magnificent Rubens ceiling and interior of Inigo Jones Banqueting House, Whitehall, circa 1622.
Department of the Environment

Heraldic beasts and ornamental towers on the Watermen's Almshouses at Penge, Kent. George Porter, 1841. *Greater London Council*

Complete renovation of Stonor Park, Oxfordshire, lived in by the family since the Norman Conquest. *Lord Camoys*

Temple of Diana, by William Chambers, at Blenheim Palace, Oxfordshire, where Winston Churchill proposed marriage. *Duke of Marlborough*

46

Dovecote, circa 1730, with 600 nesting boxes, at Cumbernauld New Town, Scotland.
Cumbernauld Development Corporation

House with unusual plasterwork, sold for five shillings in 1702. Old High Street, Hemel Hempstead. *Commission for the New Towns*

Crabble Mill, Dover, built in 1812 to provide flour for the troops, if Napoleon had invaded. *Cleary Foundation*

5. Streets for People

5. Streets for People

Shopping should be fun. It is often a nightmare. Harassed by traffic, choked by petrol fumes, pushed down badly-designed subways where steep slopes and sharp corners make it hard to negotiate a pram, or forced up elevated walkways without protection from wind and rain, housewives return home exhausted.

Contrast the joys of London Street, Norwich, where old people chat, and children play, and housewives meander, and cafes seduce you to sit and drink coffee under striped umbrellas.

In this country we owe much to Ströget, in Copenhagen, where through traffic will soon be excluded from the mediaeval town, to Essen and Cologne, to the Neuhäuserstrasse, in Munich, where you can turn the corner to the Marienplatz and hear the chimes of the clock on the famous Rathaus. I have enjoyed walking down the Kärtner-strasse, in Vienna, the mediaeval streets of Siena, the Lanes of Brighton, and Buchanan Street, Glasgow.

Pedestrianisation has many problems. Taxis, tubes, buses and car parks must be close at hand; shopkeepers will complain if there is no rear access; interesting new paving should be laid which also permits drainage of rain-water; lighting changed, seats provided, and trees or hardy shrubs introduced, not just a few tired geraniums in upturned concrete wastebins.

In this country, Leeds, Coventry, Canterbury, Liverpool, Lincoln—have succeeded. Others too, but some have failed dismally. In their so-called foot streets, buses whistle past your back, the centre is not re-paved, and traffic snarls up in the surrounding area.

I think we should also copy the nineteenth century covered markets of Leeds, Berlin or Budapest. Skelmersdale New Town have designed covered shops, perfect for their northern climate.

The separation of people, on several levels, from carriages or cars, is not a new idea. It was examined by Leonardo da Vinci, French engineers of the nineteenth century, and Le Corbusier in 'Radiant City'. However, subsequent proposals for monorails or extensive multi-level living have been rejected in our country. As we cannot fly, terra firma is preferable in reality to the tree houses of Pooh or Peter Pan, and in our streets people must have priority, or we become prisoners of our own inventions.

High Street in Old Harlow, Essex.
Harlow Development Corporation

The East End of York Minster.
Dean and Chapter

53

Town Centre, Thetford.
Norfolk County Council

High Street, Corsham, awaiting central paving, showing pedestrians still using pavements.
Wiltshire County Council

Commercial Street.
Leeds City Council

Paving of reconstituted Yorkstone and concrete buff on High Bridge, Lincoln.
Lincoln City Council

56

Cobbles and bollards in Thames Street.
Poole Borough Council, Dorset

Compass design in Albert Street.
Nottingham City Council

Workmen laying Yorkstone paving round the Bell Tower.
Dean and Chapter, Chichester Cathedral, Sussex

6. Trees, Flowers and Shrubs

The British are great gardeners. From Lands End to John-O-Groats millions of amateurs coax unwilling blooms out of unlikely soils. In the eighteenth century Lancelot Brown said everything had 'capabilities', and his sweeping vistas which highlighted the features of many historic houses illustrate the typical British approach—informal, yet disciplined. Parterres, or stylised Italian Gardens are not really cosy enough for us. The Duke of Buckingham, in the 1700s, wrote to a friend of his favourite corner: 'a little Wilderness full of blackbirds and nightingales'; Robert Baker, a rich merchant who made collars called piccadills, grew wild bugloss, pansies, and sweet william outside Piccadilla Hall, now Piccadilly Circus, and apples and pears brought over from the continent by the Earl of Lincoln in 1286, were nurtured in his well-known kitchen gardens at Lincoln's Inn.

It was the Romans who gave us *Rosa alba* and *Rosa centifolia*, and they who built elegant villas beside the Thames. The amazed Londoners, sitting on the banks fishing for salmon, saw muddy ditches transformed into colonnaded walks, and box-edged beds of hyacinths and narcissi blooming on former wasteland near Dowing Street, then Thorney Island.

Today those kitchen gardens and flower beds are blocks of flats and offices. Yet there are over ninety flowering oases in the one square mile of the City of London: hanging baskets of geraniums brighten Pinner High Street, Harrow; and Aberdeen Scotland, ablaze with miles of municipal roses, won the Britain in Bloom competition three years running.

Not only ourselves but many other countries suffer from the inevitable thorns which accompany major redevelopment. Pathetic patches of grass linger uneasily beneath constructions of towering concrete, and trees which looked healthy and mature on an architect's drawing, in reality struggle for survival in New Towns or housing estates against a hostile climate or deliberate vandalism. In Britain 80 per cent of the population live in towns and cities, so we must try to bring the country side to them.

For Heritage Year, special efforts have been made to improve Conservation Areas and the setting of old and modern buildings by planting of every kind, and the Institute of Landscape Architects have arranged seminars and an international exhibition.

But hideous overhead wires can ruin the effect of both landscaping and restoration The Electricity Boards and the Post Office have a continuous programme of under grounding but much more needs to be done.

Nowadays we may sigh for the past glories of the Mulberry Garden of James I, or search in vain for grapes in Vine Street; nevertheless trees, flowers and shrubs are burgeoning in unexpected places throughout the United Kingdom.

Rare orchids, roses, and an Italian garden are part of the setting of Dyffryn House, Wales.
Mid and South Glamorgan County Council

Work under way to restore gardens of Ham House, Surrey, to original 1672 design.
National Trust

Formal water gardens at Studley Royal, Ripon, enhancing the 18th Century Octagon Tower.
North Yorkshire County Council

Weeping willows and alders planted in the Thames.
Strand-on-the-Green Association, Middlesex

Volunteers removing clutter and planting shrubs in Flatford Lane.
East Bergholt Society, East Suffolk County Council

Daffodils planted by voluntary labour at Thorplands.
Northampton Development Corporation

Restoration of historic gardens designed by Lutyens and Gertrude Jekyll, circa 1910, Hestercombe, Somerset. *The Crown Commissioners*

Semi-mature plane trees planted in Castle Square.
Caernarvon City Council, Wales

Martin, Wiltshire, before and after.
Southern Electricity Board

Storrington, Sussex, before and after.
South Eastern Electricity Board, Post Office, West Sussex County Council, Storrington Parish Council

Houston, Renfrewshire, before and after.
South of Scotland Electricity Board

7. Cleaning and Floodlighting

Throughout Europe, the name of Malraux is associated with the cleaning of historic buildings in Paris. We have gasped at the newly revealed beauty of the Place Vendome, lit with discretion, the centre freed from traffic. The Madeleine, too, and the Place des Vosges, gave us a new insight into the spectacular results obtained by applying water at high pressure. Experiments on Notre Dame showed detergents to be a failure, as also sand-blasting in Edinburgh, which has left a pitted surface on some of the Georgian houses of the New Town. In Italy a new process of carefully applied jets of powdered glass has revealed the original jewel colours of the Carrara, Verona, and Istria marbles of the Loggetta di Sansovino. This was achieved by the British Venice in Peril Fund, and they have used the same system for Tintoretto's parish church, the Madonna dell'Orto, and San Nicolo dei Mendicoli.

In Britain, handsome Victorian and Edwardian buildings in Grey Street, Newcastle, have been cleaned and restored, and in other northern towns like Bradford and Manchester a century of industrial pollution has been washed away. Looking at the Foreign Office, by Gilbert Scott, the Tower of London, the Law Courts, and many fine government buildings, one can see some of the architectural details for the first time, and all over the country cleaning has become an important part of the restoration of our heritage.

Floodlighting often follows, and the Outdoor Lighting Awards for 1975, sponsored by the Electricity Council, Civic Trust and the Tourist Boards, have attracted hundreds of entries which include banks, churches, bridges, castles and the Gas Holder at Battersea.

The minimum energy used can often give the maximum amount of pleasure. In Salzburg, Austria, delicate and restrained lighting was used to create a fairyland out of parks and palaces for their Music Festival at Easter.

I hope that we will see more cleaning and floodlighting all over Europe, which can provide both an extra tourist attraction, and a new view of historic buildings.

The Guildhall, given by Lord Shelburne MP in 1757, restored and cleaned.
High Wycombe Borough Council, Buckinghamshire

Lisburn railway station, Northern Ireland, circa 1880, entirely renovated and cleaned.
Northern Ireland Railways

Station at Monkwearmouth, circa 1848, now a railway museum.
Metropolitan District Council of Sunderland

Parliament Street, Whitehall, London.
Department of the Environment

Queen Victoria said: 'It looks like the British Constitution'. Albert Hall, Kensington, circa 1871.
Royal Albert Hall Corporation

Pulls Ferry riverside walk.
Corporation of Norwich, Norfolk

HMS Belfast, Second World War Cruiser, now a naval museum. London Bridge.
Philips Electrical

Henry II Chantry, circa 1200, of St John's Hospital, Cirencester, Gloucestershire.
Cotswold District Council

Amalgamated House, Trinity Square, London, used as offices.
Amalgamated Investments

Fortifications of Dover Castle, dating from King John, circa 1204.
Dover District Council, Department of the Environment

8. Grandeur

Selby Abbey, Yorkshire, showing the West Front and the late Norman Door. Founded in 1070, and altered by Gilbert Scott in 1871, now entirely restored and cleaned.
Parochial Church Council, Selby

Queen Victoria's bedroom, Kensington Palace, where she lived with her mother, The Duchess of Kent, before her accession on 20 June 1837. She was woken up in this room and told that William IV had died, and that she was Queen.
Department of the Environment

Le Talbooth, Colchester, Essex, dating from 1530, features in the paintings by Constable of Dedham Vale. Now a restaurant, the partly sunken extensions are sited to blend perfectly with the old house.
Gerald Milsom

Burton Agnes Hall, Driffield, Yorkshire, designed by Robert Smithson in 1601, dates from the 12th Century. It is famous for the carved stone screen in the Great Hall, and the ghost of a murdered woman. The Long Gallery, partly destroyed in 1870, has been rebuilt, and the undulating Georgian plasterwork recreated.
Marcus Wickham-Boynton

Sainsbury's Staff canteen, an ingenious conversion from a former basement cheese store in an imposing 1910 building near Blackfriars Bridge, London.
Sainsburys

The Lower Orangery, Hampton Court, built in 1700 at the request of Queen Anne, was converted in 1974 to house nine famous pictures by Andrea Mantegna, The Triumph of Caesar. Painted between 1485 and 1495 for the Marquis of Mantua, they were afterwards bought by Charles I.
The Crown

The Cupola Room, Kensington Palace, designed by William Kent in 1722, where Queen Victoria held the first meeting of her Privy Council.
Department of the Environment

9. Films, Festivals and Fun

A few months ago, some friends from the Argentine came to stay with us in the country. They wanted to visit Luton Hoo, to see the exquisite Fabergé, Italian bronzes, Limoges enamels and English furniture. On our way home we drove through the village, and found a band playing near the church and hundreds of people watching the Morris dancing on the village green.

For Heritage Year there are not only village festivals and concerts in stately homes, but tours of famous and less known historic areas, heritage parties and weekends. Special architectural trails have been worked out for hundreds of towns and cities, and there are local exhibitions in museums and public libraries all over the country.

Films made by the BBC and Independent Television are portraying our own architecture and introducing us to some of the most fascinating places in Europe. There are films for children and by children, ones which are for popular or technical consumption, and cartoons, slides and lecture kits for schools.

The Civic Trust's Heritage Year Awards have attracted over thirteen hundred entries from Local Authorities, amenity societies, commercial undertakings, or individuals. The Coca-Cola Youth Awards, and competitions of all kinds run by local and national newspapers or private firms, have been a spur to further improvements of historic areas. Heritage Centres in redundant churches are opening in York and Chester, and at Faversham, Kent, which will show amusing and interesting features of the locality to residents and tourists. These are the first of a chain proposed throughout the country.

I am sure that the Post Office commemorative stamps and also the special coins will be admired by collectors all over the world, and we hope that many European visitors will attend the events which remind us that history can be fun, and that beautiful buildings are there for us all to enjoy.

Festival of Villages
Summer '75

WATERWAYS
CALENDAR
1975

EUROPEAN
ARCHITECTURAL
HERITAGE
YEAR

"When we build, let us think that we build for ever." — John Ruskin, The Stones of Venice

Leicester's Architectural Heritage

Exhibition: Museum & Art Gallery, New Walk

10th-30th May

10 a.m.-5.30pm

Lothian Heritage

Unique and historic
properties.
fascinating opportunity
to explore the
heritage of Edinburgh
and the Lothians.
Visit these lovely
places and savour
their value.

YARDS

JUNE

0. Youth and The Future

Disraeli once said 'The youth of a nation are the trustees of posterity'. It is interesting to recall that Marconi invented the wireless when he was twenty, Adam Smith was thirty-four when he wrote 'The Wealth of Nations', and at twenty-three Pitt was Prime Minister of England.

Nowadays the demands of modern technology and the pressures of commercial life force young people to specialise at an early age. Therefore it is particularly important that they should be taught in schools, polytechnics, and universities to appreciate their environment, to question any destruction or degradation of their own area, and to learn something of the broad spectrum of artistic achievement.

Architecture cannot be divorced from painting, landscaping, or engineering. It should not be clouded by too much theory. Men got dirt under their fingernails building the Pont du Gard or Chartres Cathedral. The vision was crystallised for us to admire, but it took hard work, not just pretty drawings. We can only show you a fraction of the hundreds of practical projects done by young people for Heritage Year. The response was tremendous from Youth Organisations. They have cleared canals, cleaned churches, turned wasteland into gardens, repaired footpaths, renovated gatehouses and tidied up villages. All over the country schoolchildren are working on trails, surveys and studies of the environment.

What will we bequeath to them? Architecturally, this is the Age of Ugliness. One can always point to notable exceptions like Itamariti in Brasilia; the General Motors or Seagram buildings in New York; Louisiana museum, Denmark; or Coventry Cathedral. But it is the everyday, bread and butter buildings which create character and individuality, in our towns and cities. It is vital that new houses, shops, offices and supermarkets blend with what already exists. This can be achieved by using the planning laws to effect positive improvements. Outstanding examples are the 'Triangle' at Cirencester, Gloucestershire; Wallis Supermarket, in Braintree, Essex; Church Lane, Sunderland; Old George Mall, Salisbury, and many parts of Norwich or Chester, and Fife or Haddington in Scotland.

The list should be much longer, but the inferior quality of new building in countless towns and cities proves that weak and feeble planning committees are worse than the wicked. The laws exist. The public have declared their support. There is no longer any excuse for wanton destruction followed by unacceptable ugliness. It is the young who will determine the future. I hope that they will learn from our mistakes and make a springboard of our successes.

Schoolchildren planting trees on Halton Lodge Estate, Runcorn New Town.
Runcorn Development Corporation

Cleaning up the River Don at Sheffield.
Community Service Volunteers

Boys helping to restore the local Recreation Ground.
Crockenhill and Swanley Boys' Club, Kent

Girls doing an historical survey of their village.
Girls' Brigade, 1st Earls Barton Company, Northamptonshire

Boys improving the Bristol Canal, Avon.
Duke of Edinburgh's Award Scheme

Young volunteers dredging the stream at Chart Gunpowder Mills, Faversham, Kent.
Faversham Society

96

Excavating at Candleston Castle, Glamorgan, Wales.
National Conservation Corps

Tidying up the churchyard, Weston Favell.
65th Girl Guides Company

Brick and timber building linking the Old Palace. Anglian Management Centre, Danbury. *Essex County Council*

Forge shopping centre, Stockton Heath—showing machinery which made ironmongery for the Manchester Ship Canal. *Warrington New Town*

Wallis supermarket, Braintree, Essex. Brilliant blending of old and new with gabled roofs.
Essex County Council

Elegant arch faced with Bath Stone fills a derelict site in Abbey Green.
Bath City Council

Interesting detail in Sandgate, Ayr.
Royal Bank of Scotland

Clever bronze and glass extension to Alfred Waterhouse's Natural History Museum, built 1880.
Department of the Environment

100

New shops in Old Church Lane, Bishopwearmouth, which linked the village green and port.
Metropolitan District Council of Sunderland

11. The European Connexion

We are not new Europeans. Our ancestors were those tribes from Central Asia who settled on the Continent of Europe, and over the centuries we have become linked not only by treaties and dynastic marriages, but by the flow of intellectual thought. Wars have divided us, or brought us together against a common enemy. Attacks of the Black Death, which decimated the population of many European countries and allowed wolves to prowl the deserted streets of Paris, showed man's impotence against elemental forces, and his amazing capacity for survival.

Conquest followed by settlement gave a temporary stability, and resulted in the growth of towns and cities. Hadrian's wall, which still straddles parts of the Pennines, and the Norman churches all over Britain, remind us of our conquerors, while through the glories of the Alhambra the Moors have left their indelible mark on Spain. In times of peace buildings were designed for use, and sometimes for show, like the Belvedere in Vienna or the Ducal Palace in Mantua. Magnificent churches and monasteries dominated Vezelay or Salzburg. In Florence the Medici vied with other rulers like Francois 1er to attract the services of architects and craftsmen such as Cellini and Michelangelo. Ideas were diffused, designs copied, new styles evolved.

When Inigo Jones went to Italy in the sixteenth century he saw the frescoes of Giorgione still fresh upon the outside walls of the Palaces in Venice. Wren met Bernini. Robert Adam, after visiting Diocletian's palace at Split, returned with bulging notebooks of architectural detail which has been copied and re-copied up to the present day. In Spain, Leon Cathedral is French Gothic, and the town hall opposite the west façade of Santiago de Compostela, was designed in 1682 by a French architect. Jean Tijou, one of the Huguenots who came to England after the Revocation of the Edict of Nantes, embellished Burghley and Drayton with his exquisite wrought ironwork. Cipriani, Artari, Zucchi; the list is endless of Italians whose delicate plasterwork and paintings enliven the ceilings and walls of great houses.

Our high streets did not escape fashionable influences. We can still admire the Stock Exchange in Glasgow, reminiscent of the Doges' Palace; Dutch gables in King's Lynn; glittering golden mosaics on Edwardian buildings in Leeds; copies of Greek friezes in Leicester; and Lloyds Bank in Bristol based on the Sansovino Library in Venice.

Hugh Trevor-Roper reminds us that it is: 'European techniques, European examples, European ideas, which have shaken the non-European world out of its past'. Today European countries need each other more than ever before. Perhaps Heritage Year can bring us closer together. Perhaps a greater appreciation of our common architectural heritage will make us value what made it possible. Peace, and an economic and cultural climate in which vision, craftsmanship, and a sense of beauty were regarded as essential in a civilised society. I hope that we Europeans can preserve and improve our legacy from the past and merge it successfully with our plans and dreams for the future.

The Golden Gates at Burghley House, Stamford, by the Huguenot Jean Tijou, circa 1699.
Marquess of Exeter

104

Ceiling detail by Cipriani, circa 1755, at Moor Park, Hertfordshire, designed by the Venetian Giacomo Leoni. *Moor Park Golf Club*

Wall painting in the Blue Boudoir at Althorp, Northamptonshire, by Pernotin, circa 1790. *Earl Spencer*

Dutch influence on Windsor Guildhall, by Wren, completed 1690, showing statue of Prince George of Denmark. *Royal Borough of Windsor and Maidenhead*

Greek Revival for the Erectheum on St Pancras Church, Euston, London, by the Inwoods, circa 1819. *The Incumbent*

The Custom House, King's Lynn, by Henry Bell, 1683, reminiscent of Hoorn and Alkmaar, Holland. *Department of the Environment*

Orangery at Bowood, Wiltshire, by Robert Adam, circa 1768, based on Emperor Diocletian's Palace at Split. *Earl of Shelburne*

Italian Gothic porch at Deene, Northamptonshire, circa 1570.
Edmund Brudenell

The End

Visits

Apart from areas already well-known to the Chairman, she made special visits to the following places:

In England

AVON Bristol, Bath
CAMBRIDGESHIRE Wisbech
CHESHIRE Chester
DERBYSHIRE Buxton, Cromford
DEVON Exeter
DORSET Poole
DURHAM Darlington
ESSEX Coggeshall, Braintree, Thaxted, Saffron Walden, Clavering
GLOUCESTERSHIRE Cirencester, Cheltenham, Tewkesbury
GREATER MANCHESTER Bolton
HAMPSHIRE Winchester, Portsmouth, Beaulieu, Bucklers Hard
HEREFORD AND WORCESTER Droitwich
KENT Faversham, Dover
LANCASHIRE Firwood Fold
LEICESTERSHIRE Leicester
LINCOLNSHIRE Lincoln, Sleaford
NORFOLK Norwich, King's Lynn
NORTHAMPTONSHIRE Duddington
NORTHUMBERLAND Alnwick
NORTH YORKSHIRE York, Richmond, Ripon, Scarborough
NOTTINGHAMSHIRE Nottingham, Wellow, Scrooby, Cossall
OXFORDSHIRE Oxford, Banbury
TYNE AND WEAR Newcastle, Sunderland, Monkwearmouth
WEST YORKSHIRE Pontefract
WILTSHIRE Corsham, Wootton Bassett

New Towns

ESSEX Harlow
HERTFORDSHIRE Welwyn, Hatfield, Hemel Hempstead, Stevenage
LANCASHIRE Skelmersdale
NORTHAMPTONSHIRE Corby
TYNE AND WEAR Washington

In Scotland

LOTHIAN REGION Edinburgh
STRATHCLYDE REGION Helensburgh, Eaglesham, Kilbarchan, Houston

In Wales

GWENT Monmouth

In Northern Ireland

The visit was cancelled due to outbreak of hostilities

Visits Abroad for seminars or meetings

FRANCE Paris
BELGIUM Brussels
SWITZERLAND Zurich, Stein-am-Rhein, and Schatthausen
DENMARK Copenhagen, Elsinore
SPAIN Madrid, Benavente, Leon, Santiago de Compostela
HOLLAND Amsterdam, The Hague
PORTUGAL Alvor

Legislation

Conservation is concerned with the integral character of an area: not only preserving individual buildings but also ensuring that any re-development respects the area's character. Conservation is part of planning law in addition to ancient monuments and historic buildings legislation. Scheduled ancient monuments are unoccupied, historic buildings normally occupied.

PRESERVATION OF, AND FINANCIAL HELP FOR, ANCIENT MONUMENTS

Under the *Ancient Monuments Acts of 1913 and 1931*, and the *Historic Buildings and Ancient Monuments Act 1953*,

(i) There are 18,000 scheduled ancient monuments, of which 759 are in the guardianship or ownership of the State;

(ii) An owner of a scheduled monument must give 3 months notice of intention to repair, alter, demolish or do any work affecting its character;

(iii) A monument in danger from neglect or injudicious treatment can be placed under the protection of the State;

(iv) Repair grants can be given to private owners of scheduled monuments.

PRESERVATION OF, AND FINANCIAL HELP FOR, HISTORIC BUILDINGS

(a) Since 1947, under successive *Town and Country Planning Acts*, nearly 235,000 buildings in England, Scotland and Wales have been listed as buildings of special architectural or historic interest.

(b) Under the *Town and Country Planning Act 1971*,

(i) No listed building can be demolished or altered without consent from the local planning authority;

(ii) If an owner fails to take reasonable steps for the preservation of a listed building, the local planning authority may serve a repairs notice specifying necessary works (and after 2 months may be authorised to compulsorily purchase the building);

(iii) The local planning authority may undertake repairs urgently necessary for the preservation of an *unoccupied* listed building and recover the cost from the owners.

(c) Under the *Town and Country Amenities Act 1974*, local planning authorities must publicise any development proposals which would affect the setting of a listed building.

(d) Under the *Historic Buildings and Ancient Monuments Act 1953*, grants are available for the repair of buildings or groups of buildings ('town schemes') of *outstanding* architectural or historic interest.

(e) Under the *Local Authorities (Historic Buildings) Act 1962*, local authorities may make grants to historic buildings, whether listed or not.

CONSERVATION AREAS (CONTROLS AND GRANTS)

Under the

Town and Country Planning Act 1971
Town and Country Planning (Amendment) Act 1972
Town and Country Amenities Act 1974

(a) local planning authorities

  (i) designate as conservation areas any 'areas of special architectural or historic interest the character or appearance of which it is desirable to preserve or enhance';
 (ii) must, if directed by the appropriate Secretary of State, formulate and publish schemes of enhancement for their conservation areas;
(iii) must have regard to the character of a conservation area when exercising their powers under the Planning Acts;
 (iv) must publicise any proposals affecting the character of the area;

(b) within the conservation area

  (i) no building (except certain small categories) can be demolished without the consent of the local planning authority;
 (ii) the powers of the local planning authority to carry out emergency repairs to an unoccupied listed building includes selected unoccupied *un*listed buildings;
(iii) there are provisions for preservation of trees and the better control of advertisements;

(c) Government grants are available for the improvement/enhancement of *outstanding* conservation areas.

Thanks from the Chairman

I am deeply grateful to:

HRH THE DUKE OF EDINBURGH for his constant interest since 1972, his informed advice, and his unfailing readiness to help in every way.

HM QUEEN ELIZABETH THE QUEEN MOTHER for presiding at our Mansion House meeting, and for her enthusiasm and encouragement.

MICHAEL MIDDLETON for his unending flow of ideas, his efficiency, his sense of humour, and for being the ideal person to work with.

JACK MUIRSHIEL and JAMES DUNBAR-NASMITH for always bringing us good news from Scotland.

LIAM MCCORMICK for his great efforts against almost overwhelming odds in Northern Ireland.

MERVYN JONES for his hard work in Wales.

STUART YOUNG for his magnificent total for our Architectural Heritage Fund.

HUGH GRAFTON for speaking on our behalf at many weekend and evening meetings.

ARTHUR KELTING for his help with New Towns and the Property Industry.

DEREK WARING for arranging a Regional Conference and for contacting so many District Councils.

WILLIE BELL for his work with the London Boroughs and the Greater London Council.

ROBIN MCCALL for advice and help with the Metropolitan Authorities.

GRAHAM ASHWORTH for his visits in the Regions.

LEONARD WOLFSON for his generosity and kindness.

ALFIE WOOD for his down-to-earth approach.

DUNCAN DUNCAN-SANDYS for his interest and support.

VIVIAN LIPMAN for being our 'Eminence grise'.

LLOYD WARBURTON for always finding time to solve our problems, and for writing the page on Conservation Legislation.

I am most indebted to the Panel Chairmen:

SANDY GLEN, Tours and Events, for arranging such an impressive list of gaieties that there is an activity for all seasons.

ASA BRIGGS, Education, for infiltrating knowledge of the environment into schools polytechnics and universities, seemingly by magic.

JOHNNIE SPENCER, Youth, for bringing together the Youth Organisations who have organised hundreds of imaginative projects to improve town and countryside.

ALFIE WOOD, Heritage Year Grants, who has been wise, and fair, in balancing de mand against supply, for the many deserving applications for our money.

PETER PARKER, Industry and Commerce, for bravely laying the trail of environ mental consciousness in the avenues of profit and loss at a time when the latter is o greater concern.

KENNETH GARLICK, Museums, for taking over from Francis Watson and for suc cessfully encouraging Museum Directors in many areas to arrange local exhibitions

PETER KING, Films and Television, for helping us to ensure that a wide variety o both will be seen during 1975.

The Panel Chairmen have been backed by panel members who have given generously of their time and expertise and I am so grateful to them all.

I would like to thank:

JULIAN AMERY, PAUL CHANNON and GEOFFREY RIPPON who kindly promoted our interests when members of the Government.

ANTHONY CROSLAND for his constructive help and personal attention to our cause

ALMA BIRK for her active support.

PETER ROBSHAW, JOHN BARROLL, GORDON MICHELL, ARTHUR PERCIVAL, KEITH EGLESTON, ROSEMARY WATT, ANNA MCPHERSON, LAURA HICKS and the staff of the Civic Trust, for their dedicated and expert work towards the protection and enhance ment of our villages, towns and cities. Their achievements are unsung—but visible up and down the country.

I want to mention especially:

SARA MOORE, my secretary, who has worked far beyond the call of duty, and been a tremendous help.

DENISE DOUGHTY-TICHBORNE, the fastest and most accurate typist imaginable, for her tireless work.

SUE PRIDEAUX for collecting some of the photographs.

DEE SMALLRIDGE for her imagination and infinite trouble in designing and preparing the layout.

BRIAN BAYLISS of the Department of the Environment and HERBERT LEADER of Her Majesty's Stationery Office for their kindness and help over printing this book.

GLENYS MCIVER of the Department of the Environment Library, for coping with the index.

My very special thanks to:

OSBERT LANCASTER for the marvellous cartoon.

ROY STRONG for his Exhibition on 'The Destruction of the Country House', his positive approach, and his original ideas which are an inspiration to us all.

PHILIPPE DE ROTHSCHILD, for generously giving up many hours of precious time to help in preparing the brilliant final version of the French text.

WALTER HARTLEY for his ingenuity in translating the poem 'Rivers' by T. Storer into German.

RONNIE GRIERSON, for his invaluable aid with the German translation, and thereby proving that the busiest people are always the most helpful and efficient.

JOHNNIE SPENCER for the stunning cover photograph, for the photographs on all the coloured papers, and for driving far afield with his camera at all hours and in all weathers to get exactly the right view of King's Lynn Customs House, Windsor Town Hall, The Tijou gates at Burghley and Drayton, the porch at Deene, the Windmill at Burnham Overy, the pier at Bangor, to mention only a few of his excellent photographs which adorn this book.

Finally, I offer heartfelt thanks to the thousands of people who have worked in their own areas and in their own way to make a success of Heritage Year, which I hope will be remembered long after 1975.

119

Acknowledgements for the Photographs

Front Cover
Arch in Priory Lane, King's Lynn, Norfolk   *The Earl Spencer*

Back Cover
Priory Cottages, King's Lynn, Norfolk   *The Earl Spencer*

Front End Paper
Detail of the Duchess of Norfolk's gate by Jean Tijou at Drayton House, Northamptonshire
The Earl Spencer

Half Title Page
Castle Combe, Dorset   *British Tourist Authority*

Title Page
Auchroisk Distillery, Fife   *Henk Snoek*

Reverse of Title Page
Bingley Locks, Bradford   *Derek Pratt*

BEFORE AND AFTER

Cover Winged Victory on the Victoria Memorial, The Mall   *The Earl Spencer*

Castle Mill, Dorking   *Peter Kingsford*
Heage Windmill, Derbyshire   *Civic Trust Heritage Year Award*
Makerstoun, Kelso   *A L Hunter*
Queen Anne Yard, Norwich   *Michael and Sheila Gooch*
Perth Waterworks   *Dr W H Findlay*
Tudor house, Exeter   *W D Lovell*
High Street, Coleshill   *Paul Barber Studios*
The Crescent, Buxton   *Middletons*
Pitcullo Castle, Fife   *R C Spence*
Lansdowne Parade, Cheltenham   *Bill Bawden*
Malt Mill Lane, Alcester   *Associated Architects, Birmingham*

DETAILS

Cover Bronze Neptune in the National Museum, Athens   *The Earl Spencer*

Staircase at Tyttenhanger House, Hertfordshire   *John S Bonnington partnership*
Chair from Hill House, Helensburgh   *Royal Commission on Ancient Monuments, Scotland*
Stone Vase on the Fowler building, Covent Garden   *Greater London Council*
Norton Priory undercroft, Runcorn   *Runcorn Development Corporation*
Tablet at the Geffrye Museum, Shoreditch   *Greater London Council*

121

The Lake Pavilion, Stowe	*Stowe School*
Staircase in Amalgamated House, City	*Photo Coverage Ltd*
Craftsman at Kenwood House, Hampstead	*Greater London Council*
Door canopies at Laurence Pountney Hill, London	*S Prideaux*
Chandelier at Crockford's Club, Westminster	*Greater London Council*

NEW USES

Cover Windmill at Burnham Overy, Norfolk	*The Earl Spencer*
West Mill, Edinburgh	*A L Hunter*
The Old Gaol, Bath	*Civic Trust Heritage Year Award*
Samlesbury Hall, Lancashire	*Civic Trust Heritage Year Award*
The Clock Flour-mill, Bromley-by-Bow	*Bass Charrington Vintners*
Exceat Farm, East Sussex	*East Sussex County Council*
Victorian Chapel, Lincoln	*P G Bartlett*
St Katherine Dock, Tower Hamlets	*Greater London Council*
The Old Town Hall, Westbury	*David Wiltshire*
The Long Room, New College, Oxford	*Civic Trust Heritage Year Award*
St Thomas Chapel, Ludlow	*South Shropshire District Council*
Kenilworth Water Tower, Warwickshire	*Civic Trust Heritage Year Award*

BEAUTY RESTORED

Cover Rigging of the Cutty Sark, Greenwich	*The Earl Spencer*
Egyptian Revival house, Penzance	*Richard Bros*
St John the Baptist Church, Liverpool	*Molyneux Photography*
The Banqueting House, Whitehall	*Department of the Environment*
Watermen's Almshouses, Penge	*Greater London Council*
Stonor Park, Oxfordshire	*Country Life*
Temple of Diana, Blenheim Palace	*British Leyland Motor Corporation*
Dovecote, Cumbernauld	*Cumbernauld News Studio*
Old High Street, Hemel Hempstead	*Commission for the New Towns*
Crabble Mill, Dover	*Roy Warner Ltd*

STREETS FOR PEOPLE

Cover Fruit shop—Alexandria, Egypt	*The Earl Spencer*
Old Harlow, Essex	*Henk Snoek*
York Minster, before and after	*York Corporation*
Town Centre, Thetford	*Norfolk County Council*
High Street, Corsham	*Civic Trust Heritage Year Award*
Commercial Street, Leeds	*City Development Office, Leeds*
Lincoln, High Street	*John S Anderson*
Thames Street, Poole	*John Harris*
Albert Street, Nottingham	*Nottingham City Council*
Chichester Cathedral, Sussex	*Thomas Photos*

TREES, FLOWERS AND SHRUBS

Cover Hibiscus Flower, Lake Como, Italy — *The Earl Spencer*

Dyffryn House, Wales	*Civic Trust Heritage Year Award*
Ham House, Surrey	*National Trust*
Studley Royal, Ripon	*North Yorkshire County Council*
Willows and alders, Strand-on-the-Green	*Civic Trust Heritage Year Award*
Flatford Lane, East Bergholt	*East Anglian Daily Times and associated papers*
Daffodil planting, Thorplands	*Northampton Development Corporation*
Hestercombe House, Somerset	*County Planning Department, Somerset County Council*
Castle Square, Caernarvon	*Terence Soames (Cardiff) Ltd*
Martin, Wiltshire, before and after	*Antony Miles Ltd*
Storrington, Sussex, before and after	*Walter Gardiner Photography*
Houston, Renfrewshire, before and after	*South of Scotland Electricity Board*

CLEANING AND FLOODLIGHTING

Cover Tower of King William Block, Greenwich Hospital — *The Earl Spencer*

The Guildhall, High Wycombe	*Colin Westwood Photography*
Lisburn Station, Northern Ireland	*Boreland Studios*
Monkwearmouth Station, Sunderland	*Civic Trust Heritage Year Award*
Parliament Street, Whitehall	*Sam Lambert*
Royal Albert Hall, Kensington	*Salisbury Photo Press*
Pulls Ferry riverside walk, Norwich	*Corporation of Norwich*
HMS Belfast, London	*Philips Electrical*
Henry II Chantry, Cirencester	*George Roper*
Amalgamated House, City	*Amalgamated Investments*
Dover Castle, Kent	*Dover District Council*

GRANDEUR

Cover Gates of Sandringham House, Norfolk — *The Earl Spencer*

Selby Abbey, Yorkshire	*Kershaw Studios*
Queen Victoria's bedroom, Kensington Palace	*Department of the Environment*
Le Talbooth, Colchester	*David L Lipsom*
Burton Agnes Hall, Driffield	*Donald I Innes*
Sainsbury's Staff canteen, Blackfriars	*Sainsburys*
The Lower Orangery, Hampton Court	*J Bethell*
The Cupola Room, Kensington Palace	*Department of the Environment*

FILMS, FESTIVALS AND FUN

Cover Pier at Bangor, North Wales — *The Earl Spencer*

Posters	*The Earl Spencer*
Coin	*The Earl Spencer*
Stamps	*The Earl Spencer*
Town Trails	*The Earl Spencer*
Morris Dancers	*British Tourist Authority*

123

YOUTH AND THE FUTURE

Cover Sculpture of Mother and Child, Ministry of Defence, Whitehall — *The Earl Spencer*

Schoolchildren planting trees, Runcorn	*Runcorn Development Corporation*
Cleaning up the River Don, Sheffield	*Community Service Volunteers*
Crockenhill and Swanley Boys' Club, Kent	*Kentish Times*
Girls' Brigade surveying their village, Northamptonshire	*Girls' Brigade*
Boys improving the Bristol Canal	*Duke of Edinburgh's Award Scheme*
Chart Gunpowder Mills, Faversham	*Kentish Observer*
Excavating at Candleston Castle, Glamorgan	*National Conservation Corps*
Churchyard, Weston Favell	*Girl Guides Association*
Old Palace, Danbury	*Essex County Council*
Forge shopping centre, Stockton Heath	*Newcombe and Johnson*
Wallis supermarket, Braintree	*Essex County Council*
St Michael's Arch, Bath	*Civic Trust Heritage Year Award*
Royal Bank of Scotland, Ayr	*George Crawford*
Natural History Museum, South Kensington	*Harry Neal*
Old Church Lane, Bishopwearmouth	*Civic Trust Heritage Year Award*

THE EUROPEAN CONNEXION

Cover Statue of Queen Victoria, High Street, Windsor — *The Earl Spencer*

The Golden Gates, Burghley House, Stamford	*The Earl Spencer*
Ceiling, Moor Park, Hertfordshire	*Richard Bryant*
Blue Boudoir, Althorp, Northamptonshire	*The Earl Spencer*
Windsor Guildhall, Berkshire	*The Earl Spencer*
St Pancras Church, Euston	*Greater London Council*
Customs House, King's Lynn, Norfolk	*The Earl Spencer*
Diocletian Wing, Bowood, Wiltshire	*Country Life*
Porch at Deene, Northamptonshire	*The Earl Spencer*

THE END

Stone Eagle at Drayton House, Northamptonshire — *The Earl Spencer*

Reverse
Dovecote at Waddesdon, Buckinghamshire — *The Earl Spencer*

Page 120
Clock Tower of the Horseguards, Whitehall — *The Earl Spencer*

Page 136
The Nile, Cairo, Egypt — *The Earl Spencer*

Page Opposite 136
Pub sign 'The Cricketers', Sarratt, Hertfordshire — *The Earl Spencer*

End Paper
The Eagle gates by Jean Tijou at Drayton House, Northamptonshire — *The Earl Spencer*

Bibliography

The poem on page 136 is from 'Poèmes élisabéthains' by Philippe de Rothschild, published by Éditions Seghers, Paris

AUTHOR	TITLE	PUBLISHER
Sacheverell Sitwell	British architects and craftsmen	Batsford
Hugh Trevor-Roper	The rise of Christian Europe	Thames & Hudson
Kenneth Clark	Civilisation	BBC & John Murray
Oscar Newman	Defensible space	Architectural Press
Peter F Smith	The dynamics of urbanism	Hutchinson Educational
Nikolaus Pevsner	Pioneers of modern design	Pelican
Nikolaus Pevsner	Buildings of Northamptonshire	Penguin
John Fergusson	The Heritage of Hellenism	Thames & Hudson
Warburg & Courtauld Institutes	England and the Mediterranean tradition	Oxford University Press
Pearl Jephcott	Homes in high flats	Oliver & Boyd
Dartmouth Report	How do you want to live?	HMSO
Homan Potterton	Irish church monuments	Ulster Architectural Heritage Society
	Do you care about historic buildings?	Greater London Council
	Streets for people	Organisation for Economic Co-operation and Development, Paris
	The conservation of historic monuments in the Federal Republic of Germany	Inter Nationes Bonn—Bad Godesberg
John Fowler John Cornforth	English decoration in the 18th century	Barrie & Jenkins
W R Dalzell	Architecture	Hamlyn
Benvenuto Cellini	Autobiography	Penguin
Philippe Erlanger	Charles VII et son mystère	Editions Gallimard
Christopher Hibbert	The rise and fall of the House of Medici	Allen Lane

AUTHOR	TITLE	PUBLISHER

and
Publications for Heritage Year

Tony Aldous	A place in Europe (book of Thames TV series)	Phoebus
Colin Amery, ed	Period houses and their details	Architectural Press
Julian Barnard	The decorative tradition	Architectural Press
Bedfordshire County Council	Bedfordshire historical buildings	Bedfordshire County Planning Department
M Binney and A Emery	Architectural guide to Penshurst Place	ABC Historic Publications
C E B Brett	Buildings of St Peter Port	National Trust of Guernsey
British Tourist Authority	Britain: European Architectural Heritage Year 1975	British Tourist Authority
British Tourist Authority	Britain: town trails	British Tourist Authority
British Tourist Boards	Resorts and spas in Britain	British Tourist Authority
Dorothy Brown	Bristol and how it grew	Bristol Visual and Environmental Group
London Borough of Camden	Heritage Year in Bloomsbury	London Borough of Camden
Sherban Cantacuzino, ed	Architectural conservation in Europe	Architectural Press
Sherban Cantacuzino, ed	New uses for old buildings	Architectural Press
Cheshire County Council	Cheshire—your heritage	Cheshire County Planning Department
Civic Trust	Heritage Year Awards Report	Civic Trust
Civic Trust & National Book League	Books on historical buildings and places	National Book League
Peter Collymore	House conversion	Architectural Press
John Cornforth	Country houses in Britain— can they survive?	British Tourist Authority
Clare Crick	Victorian buildings in Bristol	Bristol & West Building Society
Dan Cruickshank Peter Wyld	London: the art of Georgian buildings	Architectural Press
Gillian Darley	Villages of vision	Architectural Press
Department of the Environment with London Borough of Greenwich	Greenwich in European Architectural Heritage Year	London Borough of Greenwich

126

AUTHOR	TITLE	PUBLISHER
Department of the Environment Yorkshire & Humberside Region	Positive urban conservation	Department of the Environment Yorkshire & Humberside Region
Fife County Council	Architectural trail through Fife	Fife County Council
Brian Goodey	Urban walks and town trails	Birmingham University Centre for Urban & Regional Studies
Haslemere Estates	Something more of London restored	Carlos Press
Borough of Havant	Conserving your heritage	Havant Borough Council
Edward Jacob	History of Faversham (1774; 1975 reprint)	Faversham Society
Paul Johnson	A place in history (book of Thames TV series)	Weidenfeld and Nicolson
Royal Borough of Kensington & Chelsea	Your architectural heritage: a book list with a section on Kensington & Chelsea	Kensington & Chelsea Libraries Service
Leicester City Council	Leicester's architectural heritage	Leicester City Planning Department
Leicestershire Libraries & Information Service	Architectural heritage: a guide to resources	Leicestershire County Library Service
City of Lincoln	Planning problems in historic cities and towns	Lincoln Department of Planning & Architecture
Bryan Little	Sir Christopher Wren	Robert Hale Limited
David W Lloyd	The buildings of Portsmouth and its environs	City of Portsmouth
Nathaniel Lloyd	A history of the English house (1931; 1975 reprint)	Architectural Press
Duncan McAra	Sir James Gowans	Paul Harris Publishing
George Mansell, ed, with J M Hirsh	The living heritage of Westminster	Westminster City Council, Westminster Chamber of Commerce, Cities of London & Westminster Society of Architects
National Council of Social Service	'Make a trail . . .'	National Council of Social Service
National Trust for Scotland	Little Houses in Fife	National Trust for Scotland
City of Oxford	Conservation in Oxford	Oxford City Department of Architecture & Planning

AUTHOR	TITLE	PUBLISHER
Alexander Papageorgiou	Continuity and change (1971; price reduced for 1975)	Phaidon Press
City of Plymouth	European Architectural Heritage Year	Plymouth City Planning Department
John Prizeman	Your house: the outside view	Hutchinson
Renfrew County Council	Renfrewshire heritage	Renfrew County Planning & Engineering Department
Alistair Service, ed	Edwardian architecture & its origins	Architectural Press
P Shaffrey	The Irish town: an approach to survival	Architectural Press
Staffordshire & Worcestershire Canal Society	Report on the erosion of items of historic and architectural merit	Staffordshire & Worcestershire Canal Society
H E C Stapleton et al	A skilful master builder	William Anelay Limited
Roy Strong et al	The destruction of the country house 1875–1975	Thames & Hudson
Sunderland Public Libraries	Finding out about European Architectural Heritage Year	Sunderland Public Libraries
Ray Taylor et al, eds	Britain's planning heritage	Croom Helm
Barry Turner	A place in the country (book of Thames TV series)	Weidenfeld & Nicolson
Unesco	The conservation of cities	Croom Helm
Wales Tourist Board	Castles and historic places in Wales	HMSO
A J Wallis	Dorset bridges—a history and guide	Abbey Press, Sherborne
Lance Wright, ed	A future for Dublin	Architectural Press

Index

Page numbers in *italics* refer to illustrations

Vanbrugh, John
  Castle Howard, 20
  Lake Pavilion, Stowe, *26*
Venice, 70, 102
Venice in Peril fund
  cleaning of marble, 70
Vezelay, 102
Victoria, *Queen of Great Britain*
  bedroom, Kensington Palace, *82*
  opinion of Albert Hall, *73*
Victorian period
  Albert Hall, *73*
  chapel, Lincoln, *34–5*
  church of St John the Baptist,
    Liverpool (Bodley), 40, *42*
  Covent Garden, *23*
  exterior of Adam house, *6*
  Foreign Office, 70
  Leeds covered market, 50
  Lisburn railway station, *72*
  Monkwearmouth station, 2, *72*
  Newcastle upon Tyne, 70
  Perth Waterworks, 2, *8–9*
  stone windmill, Heage, *4–5*
  Tower House, Kensington, 20
  Watermen's Almshouses, Penge, 40,
    44
Vienna, 50, 102
Vine Street, 60

Volunteers in conservation, xi, 92, *93,*
  94, 95, 96

Wallis supermarket, Braintree, 92, *98*
Waterhouse, Alfred
  Natural History Museum, *99*
Watermen's Almshouses, Penge, 40, *44*
West Mill, Edinburgh, *31*
Westbury
  Old Town Hall, *36*
Weston Favell, *96*
Whitehall, 40, *43, 73*
Windmills, *4–5, 38*
Windsor
  Guildhall, *105*
Wren, *Sir* Christopher, 102
  Windsor Guildhall, *105*
Wurzburg, 20

York, xi, 86
  Minster, *52*
Youth
  see Education

Zucchi, Antonio, 20, 102

Printed in England for Her Majesty's Stationery Office
by McCorquodale Printers Ltd, London
Dd 289334   K56   9/75

RIVERS

Fair Danubie is praised for being wide;
Nilus commended for the sevenfold head;
Euphrates for the swiftness of the tide,
And for the garden whence his course is led;
The banks of the Rhine with vines are overspread:
Take Loire and Po, yet all may not compare
With English Thamesis for buildings rare.

By Thomas Storer 1571-1604

HER MAJESTY'S STATIONERY OFFICE

Government Bookshops

49 High Holborn, London WC1V 6HB
13a Castle Street, Edinburgh EH2 3AR
41 The Hayes, Cardiff CF1 1JW
Brazennose Street, Manchester M60 8AS
Southey House, Wine Street, Bristol BS1 2BQ
258 Broad Street, Birmingham B1 2HE
80 Chichester Street, Belfast BT1 4JY

*Government publications are also available
through booksellers*

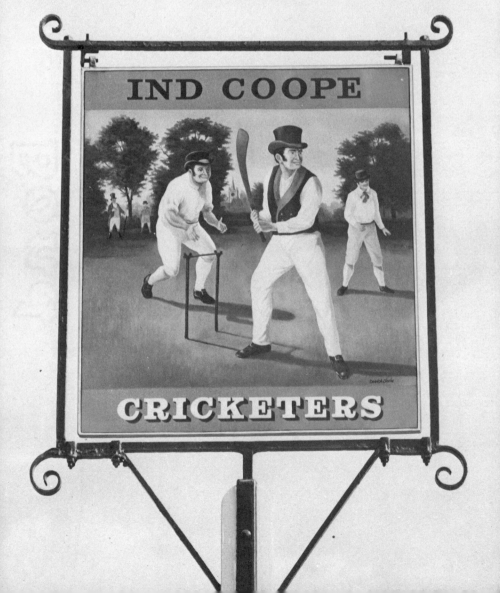